LIVING DANGEROUSLY

DANGEROUSLY

DIVERS

KENDALL McDONALD

LIVING **DANGEROUSLY**

ASTRONAUTS

DIVERS

FIREFIGHTERS

PILOTS

RACING DRIVERS

STUNT PERFORMERS

Series Editor: James Kerr
Designers: Helen White, Jackie Berry

Cover: Diving on a sunken wreck off the coast of Cuba.

First published in 1991 by Wayland (Publishers) Limited,
61 Western Road, Hove, East Sussex BN3 1JD

British Library Cataloguing in Publication Data
McDonald, Kendall
   Divers. – (Living dangerously)
   I. Title II. Series
   627.023

HARDBACK ISBN 0-7502-0112-6

PAPERBACK ISBN 0-7502-0474-5

Typeset by Dorchester Typesetting Group Limited.
Printed in Italy by G. Canale & C.S.p.A., Turin.
Bound in Belgium by Casterman, S.A.

CONTENTS

THE DIVING BOOM

LEFT Divers can now join the fish in the deep sea.

If you have ever looked at the surface of the sea and wondered what it is like down below, then maybe diving is the job for you. Diving is exciting, which is why scuba diving is the fastest-growing sport in Britain – and probably the whole world.

Mind you, it was only a few years ago that a black-suited diver standing on a beach with his or her air bottles and other equipment would cause a crowd to gather. Today, men and women sport divers wearing multicoloured suits in their fast inflatable-boats are a familiar sight around coasts throughout the world.

BELOW Fish are often bold enough to take food from a diver's hands.

Even though this sight is taken for granted, divers are still regarded as daredevils. Divers have always been thought – by non-divers – to live dangerously, risking all in day-to-day encounters under the waves with huge sharks, giants octopuses and other monsters of the deep. Today, divers are featured in books, films and television programmes all over the world. We have been able to watch underwater archaeologists carefully uncovering the cargoes of ancient ships, marine biologists showing us how corals grow on a tropical reef, or underwater photographers recording unusual kinds of fish.

Breath-hold diving is still practised by people who catch tuna in the Pacific Ocean.

With breathing equipment, sunken ships can be explored by divers.

We shall never know the name of the first diver, nor what drove him or her to explore underwater. We do know that by the time of the Greeks and Romans, diving was an honoured profession. Divers brought up food, pearls, red coral, sponges and sea-snails. The sea-snails were boiled to produce purple dye, which was used to colour cloth. However, it was greed which drove diving on. As the years passed, divers became mainly concerned with raising treasure from sunken ships. But these divers were still only breath-hold diving. Lots of divers died because they held their breath for so long that they became unconscious and drowned. In spite of this, great treasures were recovered. For example, William Phips was knighted by King James II of England because he brought up £2 million in gold and silver from a wrecked Spanish galleon south of the Bahamas. Nobody seemed to care that 60 local divers died in the raising of the treasure. After all, they said, everyone knows diving is a dangerous business.

Divers have recovered treasure from long-lost ships.

It was not until the nineteenth century, when the diving suit was invented, that divers could stay underwater and move around for a reasonable amount of time. The inventor of the suit, John Deane, and his brother went into wreck diving in a big way and made a good living. They were the first to dive on the wreck of Henry VIII's battleship, *Mary Rose*, sunk in 1545 off the coast of Portsmouth.

Deane's diving suit was improved by Augustus Siebe. From 1837 onward, the Siebe 'hard hat' diving apparatus, with its huge lead-soled boots and rubber hose leading from an air pump to a big, round brass helmet, was used for serious diving work all over the world. It is still in use today.

THE CRUEL SEA

Under the Antarctic ice: divers must be on ropes so that they can get back to the entry hole cut through the thick ice.

People call the sea 'cruel' or 'angry'. But as Canadian oceanographer and under-ice diving expert Joe MacInnis says, the truth is that the sea doesn't know you're there! This doesn't make the sea any less dangerous. It is hazardous because you have to take your own breathing gas down with you when you dive in. The sea is rather like outer space because there isn't any air to breathe. This is one of the reasons why the sea is often called 'inner space'.

There is another similarity between inner and outer space – the weightlessness both divers and astronauts experience. All US astronauts are trained sport divers and most do training for spacewalks in a huge water-filled tank at the Marshall Space Flight Center in Huntsville, Alabama.

Sport diving is the way into professional diving. In Britain, the professional diver training schools insist on the trainee holding a British Sub-Aqua Club Sport Diver qualification. In the USA, such schools ask to see a C-card as proof of some diving experience. And in Australia, similar proof of diving interest is required.

ABOVE Professional diving is hard work. This diver is clearing marine growth off the legs of an oil platform.

RIGHT Divers use hand signals to communicate with each other.

FAR RIGHT The sea-bed is not always flat sand or mud. Divers have to contend with piles of boulders on the Scottish sea-bed.

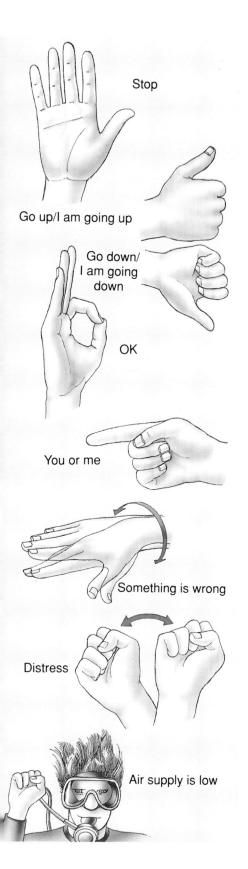

Stop

Go up/I am going up

Go down/
I am going
down

OK

You or me

Something is wrong

Distress

Air supply is low

Training professional divers is a very serious business. Putting divers down to great depths for oil drilling or pipeline work costs an enormous amount of money. The deeper the divers go, the more it costs.

Most North Sea oil diving is considered fairly shallow at around 140 m. To the west of the Shetlands, it gets deeper, with divers working at 200 m. Much of the rig diving in the Gulf of Mexico is fairly shallow, but it is getting deeper as the drillers move further offshore. Some work is going on at near the 300 m mark. A record depth for professional divers in the open sea has been set by the huge French diving company Comex, with dives to 600 m. At this sort of depth it only needs something small to go wrong and the divers could die instantly. No wonder the top divers earn more than £30,000 per year!

Before a diver starts commercial training, he or she must pass a very strict medical. A history of chest trouble will finish the diver's career before it starts. So will diabetes, ear or eye trouble, and drink or drug addiction. Colour blindness will not necessarily stop someone becoming a professional diver. All colours disappear at great depths; for example bright red looks black at 30 m, even in clear water.

Diving is hard, tough work. A diver should be at least eighteen years old before he or she starts a commercial diving course. There is no height limit, but a person must be strong enough to look after his or her diving 'buddies' if things go wrong deep down. Diving is not confined to men. Many women are sport divers and some have passed the tough commercial courses and worked on oil platforms. Most of the women in diving are in the science field. Age comes into diving. Anyone older than twenty-five would not be accepted for training if they wished to dive to great depths, breathing the mixed gases required for work down there. The mixed-gas diver's career is usually over by the age of forty.

Danger Fact

North Sea oil operations started in the 1960s and by 1974 there were 800 divers working on the European Continental Shelf. But in that one year alone, ten divers died – which meant that each diver had a one-in-eighty chance of being killed while diving.

SCIENCE **DIVING**

Not all divers want to dive for oil – some go for gold. In fact, many of the deep-diving skills pioneered during the race for oil from under the sea are used by salvage firms to bring up the cargoes of long-lost ships.

Not all non-sport diving takes place in the deep sea. From the ranks of the sport divers, estimated to be some 50,000 in Britain and over 1.5 million in the USA, have come a new breed – the science divers. They use lightweight sport diving gear; fins on their feet, masks over their noses and eyes, and neoprene suits to keep warm.

The modern underwater explorer uses a dive computer on his or her wrist.

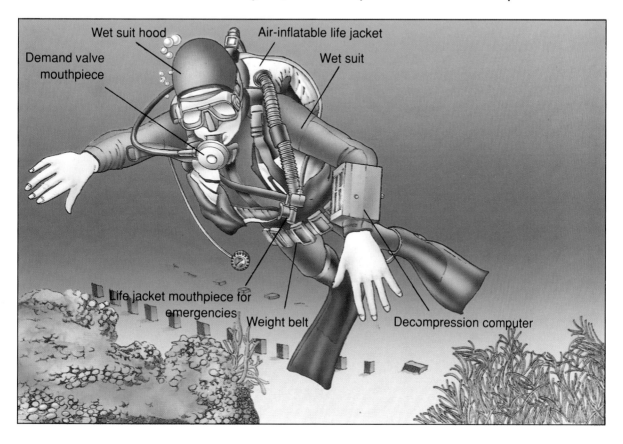

Wet suit hood

Demand valve mouthpiece

Air-inflatable life jacket

Wet suit

Life jacket mouthpiece for emergencies

Weight belt

Decompression computer

They breathe compressed air through the demand valve, invented by Jacques-Yves Cousteau, from the tanks on their backs. This kind of equipment is not recommended for use below 50 m but it is ideal for diving scientists.

There are now diving archaeologists, marine biologists, diving marine-conservationists, underwater geologists and underwater photographers at work in the shallow seas all over the world. It is in these fields that women divers really come into their own. In the USA, you'll find the world's most famous woman underwater biologist. Born in New Jersey, Dr Sylvia Earle can also lay claim to the title

Photographing corals in tropical waters.

Underwater archaeologists use a frame to plot the exact position of objects on an ancient shipwreck.

of the world's deepest woman diver! She led a team of women scientists who lived in an underwater house for two weeks, carrying out special studies in the sea off St John in the Virgin Islands of the USA. Later, wearing a special pressurized diving suit, she rode on the outside of a mini-submarine down to the sea-bed at 381 m, off the coast of Hawaii. Once there, she walked about for two-and-a-half hours on the sea floor, studying the deep-sea marine life.

Whether they are men or women, all divers are prone to the same risks and dangers when exploring underwater. Any kind of diving can be dangerous, and diving using air has special risks. One of the most common causes of accidents to divers is staying down deep too long and coming up too fast. A diver who does this will almost certainly get the 'bends'.

The 'bends'

The 'bends' is the diver's name for decompression sickness. What happens is this: as a diver is swimming along deep down, his or her blood is absorbing nitrogen from the air supply he or she is breathing. Air is made up of 78 per cent nitrogen and 21 per cent oxygen with a touch of other gases such as carbon dioxide. But it is nitrogen which is the diving danger. When the diver starts to come up, the nitrogen in the blood starts to form bubbles. It's rather like the way bubbles appear in a bottle of lemonade when you take the cap off. In fact, opening a bottle of fizzy drink is a good example of what happens to the diver. When you take the cap off, you reduce the pressure on the lemonade and out come

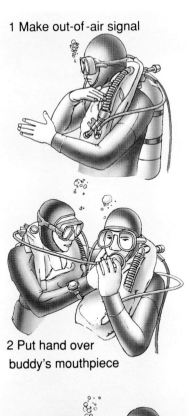

1 Make out-of-air signal

2 Put hand over buddy's mouthpiece

3 Take two breaths only

LEFT **To avoid the deadly 'bends', a diver waits on the anchor line for the nitrogen bubbles to leave his blood.**

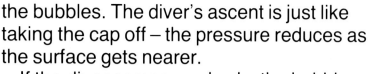
4 Return mouthpiece to buddy, who takes two breaths

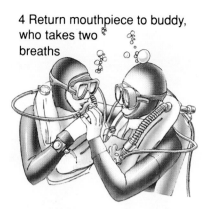

A scuba diver can get air from his or her buddy in an emergency. This is called buddy breathing.

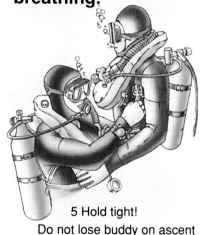

5 Hold tight!
Do not lose buddy on ascent

the bubbles. The diver's ascent is just like taking the cap off – the pressure reduces as the surface gets nearer.

If the diver comes up slowly, the bubbles remain small and are flushed out of the blood by breathing. But if he or she comes up too fast, the nitrogen starts to make bigger and bigger bubbles. The big bubbles get stuck at the diver's joints, cause intense pain and make the joints 'bend', whether the diver wants them to or not. A diver with the 'bends' can be paralyzed from the waist down if a big bubble lodges in the spine, or can be killed if a bubble damages the heart. The only cure for the 'bends' is to put the diver into a decompression chamber, increase the pressure to that of the depths and then very slowly reduce the pressure to that of the surface.

Divers use special decompression tables to tell them how long they can stay at a certain depth and how slowly to come to the surface. A very deep dive will often mean waiting at fixed depths near the surface for a long time, until the nitrogen is cleared from the body.

Danger Facts

• Decompression sickness is the most common cause of accidents to divers.
• In Britain in 1989, there were 137 cases among the 50,000 amateur divers.
• In the USA in 1989, there were 600 cases among the 1.5 million sport divers.

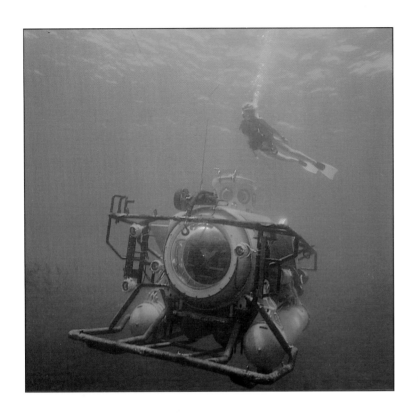

Small submarines are used to probe deeper than divers dare to go.

With such terrible problems being caused by nitrogen, why do divers bother to dive with air at all? Why don't they just use oxygen? This is what the early undersea explorers such as Hans Hass did. And it is what the Second World War frogmen did when they placed mines on the hulls of enemy ships. However, Hans Hass and the frogmen soon found out that oxygen had one terrible disadvantage. Pure oxygen when breathed more than 6-8 m under the sea is poisonous! When under the pressure of the sea below that depth it can produce sudden unconsciousness, or fits, with death following close behind.

Divers discovered that there was another problem with air. The deeper divers went, the more they were affected by a sort of drunkenness. Divers became careless, went on down when they should have come up, and even gave their mouthpieces to fish! This was yet another problem with nitrogen. Officially it was called 'nitrogen narcosis', but Cousteau called it 'rapture of the depths'. A solution to this problem was found when nitrogen was swapped for helium. However, deep-sea divers could still only stay down for short periods of time, because helium also required a long decompression.

It was an American who made the breakthrough which makes all of today's deep diving possible. 'Papa Topside' is what US Navy divers called Captain George Bond. Dr Bond was the first person to put forward the idea of 'undersea living'.

Aquanauts lived in this underwater house off the Bahamas for a fortnight at a time.

His idea was this – if you feed a gas mixture to a diver at depth, his or her body will become saturated with that gas and will not take in any more. So once that saturation point had been reached, the time it took to bring the diver back to the surface didn't take any longer, no matter how long he or she stayed down.

Dr Bond's idea worked. Cousteau kept his divers in an undersea house he called *Conshelf* for days at a time. And the USA put down two undersea living quarters. *Sealab I* was at 59 m down off the coast of Bermuda, and 'aquanauts' lived in it for ten days. *Sealab II* was down deeper in the colder waters off the coast of California at 63 m. Leader of the team of divers who spent thirty days in *Sealab II* was Scott Carpenter, astronaut turned aquanaut. Dolphins acted as 'messenger boys' carrying messages from *Sealab II* to the surface – no diving problems for them!

On the outside looking in: Dr Sylvia Earle shows a rare seaweed specimen to another woman aquanaut inside their underwater 'home' off the Virgin Islands.

SHARK!

Sharks bite! This diver wore a chain mail suit to protect him against a shark attack. This picture shows what a wise move that was!

A diver must never hold his or her breath when coming up from a dive using any kind of breathing apparatus. If he or she does so, an 'air embolism' is likely to be the result. It is simpler to call this diving danger a 'burst lung'. It happens when the gas inside the lungs expands on ascent. If the gas cannot escape from the diver's mouth, it will cause terrible damage and will probably kill the diver.

Not all diving dangers come from the gas divers breathe. Though most of the creatures of the sea are timid and usually flee from divers (who tend to make a lot more noise underwater than anything which lives there) some can turn very nasty.

The first creatures that non-divers think about are sharks. And let's face it, divers think about them too! There is nothing like the appearance of a big shark close to divers to send up their breathing rates! Divers have certainly been attacked by sharks, but the sharks usually only do so if the divers have been spear-fishing and there is fish blood in the water.

However, a possible exception to the rule is the massive species called the Great White. All sharks must be treated by divers as dangerous, but the Great White may attack without provocation. Specialists in filming these monsters are Australians Valerie and Ron Taylor, whose underwater photography, particularly of sharks, has made them famous all over the diving

Shark bait! A display of handfeeding to sharks, put on for tourist divers in the Maldives.

Moray eels look fearsome, but rarely attack divers.

world. Valerie has been bitten twice by smaller sharks. This hasn't stopped her from taking part in the Great White shark sequences for such well-known films as *Jaws* and *Blue Water, White Death*. On a shark filming expedition off the coast of South Australia, one huge Great White tried so hard to get at the Taylors, who were in a protective cage, that it bent the bars! Not all sharks are like that – or no diver would dare go in the sea. In fact, some diving holidays offer sport divers the opportunity to film special sessions where sharks are hand-fed by local divers!

What then of the octopus, called the sea-devil from the earliest of times? Well, it was diving which put paid to the 'killer' reputation of the so-called giant octopus of Hollywood films. Divers in the Mediterranean found the octopuses there weighed only a kilogram or two, and measured at most 2 m from tentacle tip to tip. And even in the chilly waters of Puget Sound in the US state of Washington, where octopuses grow to over 6 m from tip to tip, divers have stroked them and found them to be timid and gentle giants. Only one octopus is really dangerous and that is the Australian blue-ringed variety. Although it is tiny – usually less than 10 cm across – its bite is more poisonous than that of any land animal, and death often results.

Divers working on oil platforms in warm seas often report sea snakes twining themselves around their masks or arms, but few bites on divers have been reported.

There are fifty different kinds of snakes and some grow up to 2 m long. The venom of a sea snake is said to be ten times as poisonous as that of a cobra. Even so, divers in warm seas tend to treat them as all in the day's work and say that if you keep still, they will go away!

There are two other dangers for divers in warm waters. One is the deadly sting of the stonefish, which gets its name from looking like, and staying as still as, a stone. The other is the lionfish, whose back spines act like hypodermic needles, driving poison upwards into its prey. The stings of both fish produce agonizing pain, and can kill.

This woman is playing with fire! This fish, known as a lionfish or firefish, can inject a deadly poison from the spines on its back.

THE DEEP-SEA DIVER

A working day in a saturation or 'sat' diver's life starts at dawn at a mainland heliport. During the flight out to the drilling rig, all the divers aboard wear special survival suits, just in case the helicopter has to make a forced landing in the cold sea.

No time is wasted when the helicopter touches down on the rig's helipad. The divers go straight into one of the big steel decompression chambers on the rig's deck. The air pressure inside the chamber is increased. It is made equal to the pressure the divers will experience working deep

A small decompression chamber on a North Sea oil rig. This one is for short stays. Saturation divers use much bigger ones.

down. The divers then move into their living quarters. Each one grabs a bed, for they may be under pressure for as long as twenty-eight days. The divers are rarely in the chamber for longer than this. This is because no one knows if long exposure to pressure will bring health troubles later in the divers' lives.

When it is time for the divers to go to work, three put on their heated suits and their helmets and move through a hatch into the diving bell, which is clamped on to the side of the main chambers. They close the hatch behind them and connect themselves into the main supply of mixed gases. Then the bell is detached from the deck chamber and swung by crane over the 'moon pool' – a special hole in the deck – and lowered down to the sea-bed. Once in position, the divers open the bottom hatch of the bell. The sea does not come in because of the pressure in the bell. Two of the divers swim

LEFT AND RIGHT What a way to go to work! Divers travel down to the sea-bed in a bell and then swim out to carry out their jobs under the oil rig platform.

out on the ends of their 'umbilical' lines, which carry voice communications, their breathing gas, hot water for their suits and power for any tools or lights they are using. The third diver – the bellman – stays in the bell to feed out their lines and see they don't get caught up. It is the bellman's job to rescue the divers if anything goes wrong. The bellman has a winch inside the bell to pull the other divers back in. He can see the divers at work in the lights from the bell. All around the sea is black. At depths which 'sat' divers work at, no surface light reaches the sea-bed. The divers are also being watched from the control room high above on the drilling rig. Their every move is monitored, as are the vital supplies to the bell.

Divers' jobs on a drilling rig are many and varied. They may be called upon to help position the 'blow-out preventer'. This is put in to stop mud, oil and gas blowing out of the well before the drillers are ready. Divers are also called upon to fix new anchoring wires, or build a protective wall of sandbags around the legs of a rig in an area where there are strong currents. All these jobs are hard and tiring.

A 'bell run' – that is the time from leaving the surface of the sea to arriving back there again – is not allowed to be more than eight hours. This means that the divers will usually work four-hour shifts outside the bell. When their time is up, the divers return to the bell, the hatch is closed and the ascent to the surface begins. The lift through the waves near the surface can be

A professional 'sat' diver has to carry out many tasks – welding underwater is just one of them.

Diving is cold and tiring and can be dangerous unless safety rules are strictly followed.

very bumpy and all the divers are happier when the bell is clamped back again to the deck chamber. When they have got back into the living quarters, another three divers take their place and continue the work on the sea-bed. Nine divers in the saturation team means that work goes on for twenty-four hours at a time. There are risks in diving and divers know this – but the exploration of 'inner space' is exciting, and their work under the sea must go on.

GLOSSARY

Aquanauts   Divers who spend long periods of time working underwater.

Bends   A name for decompression sickness which describes the way the victim's joints bend to ease the pain. It is also called the 'chokes' or the 'staggers'.

C-card   A card issued by a US diver training agency to show the standard reached by a diver.

Compressed air   Air that has been squeezed so that it takes up less space than air at normal pressure.

Continental shelf   The sea-bed surrounding a continent.

Decompression   Returning to a condition of normal air pressure.

Decompression chamber   A steel chamber inside which pressure can be altered at will. It is used to return divers from abnormal pressures under the sea to normal air pressure.

Decompression tables   Scientific tables drawn up to show divers how to avoid the 'bends'. This is done by coming up slowly and by making timed stays at fixed depths on the way to the surface.

Demand valve   This supplies air at the correct pressure for the depth the diver is at, when he or she inhales. It is usually called a regulator in the USA.

Diving bell   A pressurized chamber in which divers are lowered to work in deep water.

Heliport   An airport for helicopters.

Marine biologist   Someone who studies animal and plant life in the sea.

Marine conservationist   Someone who works to protect animal and plant life at sea.

Mixed gas   A mixture of gases – for example helium and oxygen – which divers breathe underwater.

Moon pool   A hole in the bottom of a ship or the deck of a drilling platform which allows a diving bell to be lowered into the sea.

Neoprene   A synthetic waterproof material.

Oceanographer   Someone who studies the physical and biological features of the sea.

Saturated   Containing the maximum amount of gas possible.

Saturation ('sat') diving   Where the diver's body is completely saturated with dissolved gas, so that decompression will take the same amount of time, no matter how long the diver stays down.

Scuba A piece of equipment used for sport diving. It consists of a cylinder (or cylinders) containing compressed air which the diver breathes through a mouthpiece.

Underwater archaeologist Someone who studies historical objects and remains, buried under the sea-bed.

Underwater geologist Someone who studies the sea-bed and its rock formations.

BOOKS TO READ

Divers and Diving by Reg Vallintine (Blandford, 1981)
Exploring the Sea by Daniel Rogers (Wayland, 1991)
Snorkelling For All (British Sub-Aqua Club Manual) Edited by Mike Holbrook (Stanley Paul, 1991)
Sport Diving (The British Sub-Aqua Club Diving Manual) (Stanley Paul, 1985)
The Mary Rose by Margaret Rule (Conway Maritime Press, 1982)
The Treasure Divers by Kendall McDonald (Pelham, 1980)
The Young Scientist Book of the Undersea by C. Pick (Usborne, 1991)
Undersea Machines by R. J. Stephens (Franklin Watts, 1986)
Undersea Technology by Dr Ralph Rayner (Wayland, 1990)

ACKNOWLEDGEMENTS

The Publisher would like to thank the following for providing the illustrations in this book: British Petroleum 26, 27; The British Sub-Aqua Club (Mike Wong) 4; Bruce Coleman Limited (John Murray) 16, (Timothy O'Keefe) 18, (Jack Stein Grove) 6; Oxford Scientific Films (Doug Allen/OSF) 9, (Laurence Gould/OSF) 15, (Kim Westerkov/OSF) 5; Planet Earth Pictures (Kurt Amsler) 19, 23, (Leo Collier) 14, (Jon Kenfield) 10, 28, (Slava Rossii) 8, (Flip Shulke) 20, (Peter Scoones) COVER, 7, 25, (Marty Snyderman) 21, (Herwarth Voigtmann) 22, 24; Survival Anglia (Rick Price) 11; Wayland Picture Library 29.

The colour artwork is by the Hayward Art Group. The black and white artwork is by John Yates.

INDEX

The numbers in **bold**
refer to captions.